# An Almanac
# for Twilight

JACK MATTHEWS

THE UNIVERSITY OF NORTH CAROLINA PRESS

CHAPEL HILL                                      1966

# CONTEMPORARY POETRY SERIES

Copyright © 1958, 1959, 1960, 1961, 1962, 1963, 1964, 1965, 1966 *by* *Jack Matthews*

"Montana Night at Twenty Below" and "Remembered" originally appeared in *Poetry*. Other poems in this book have previously appeared in *The Nation, The National Review, The New Republic, The New York Times, The New York Herald Tribune, The Antioch Review, Commonweal, Discourse, The Georgia Review, Mademoiselle, The Minnesota Review,* and *The Southwest Review*.

*Library of Congress Catalog Card Number 66-15509*

*Printed by The North Carolina State University Print Shop, Raleigh*
*Manufactured in the United States of America*

*For my family*

# Contents

*An Almanac*
*for Twilight*

## Paradigm of a Hero

One memory I have from childhood
is this: a heavy man trudging
in boots, ahead of me, a lantern
bumping at his knee. I remember
stepping over railroad ties
and staring at his broad back
as he walked ahead; I remember
the smoky wake of his tobacco,
the sound of his boots clomping
in the cinders, remember tiredness,
the smell of lateness in the night . . .
I remember the darkness
which each step spilled him into,
though I forget who he was,
or why we were walking
on that cold night. I remember
the warm lantern clanking
against his leg, the darkness
all around, and the fact that
he never once paused, but stepped
like God himself, forward
into nothing, and into the past,
swinging his own casual light.

# The Catfish

I spent afternoons like an old man's drowsy years,
fishing the creek water, as frothed and gold as lager,
catching river cats beyond the ironwood spears.
But with every catch, I hoped there was another, bigger.

And began to think there was a king of catfish there,
inert as a sack of coins in the bottom mud, wise
as he meditated in his dream-dark lair,
from a tarbucket head and two pale green eyes.

From a study of the specimens expiring on the bank,
I formed a picture of the mammoth one: grumpy, old,
heavy as a tub of cheese, uncleansed by water, rank.
He oared himself erect inside my mind and glowed.

His skin was twisted like a woman's hose upon his sides,
his mouth was tasseled like a lamp with ancient hooks;
now this embodied silence simply lasts beneath the tides
as remote from baits and lures as from the flight of ducks.

I've thought upon my monster beyond the range
of credulity; accepted him as if he really existed
and shook the abutments of my reason. Beyond change,
in a myth beyond begetting, this thing has lasted.

The real ones, I have found, are mortal in the mind
as in the world of hooks and worms and lethal boys.
The dreamed one lasts on where he's never been,
untroubled as a star by hooks and facts and other toys.

## From the Uncertainty
## of Our Dire Predictions .

Apples, like a thousand children, are slaughtered
by the dark frosts that blow from the creek
and nicely pinch the stem. They fall thud
from the still cider air into thistles

tangled like green starfish on the ground;
and there will be not sun enough
and flies, fat bees and wasps enough
to brown the fruit into small circles

of garbage in the thistle's cradle
(what the thoughtless cattle haven't eaten,
and the wild deer that stalk beyond sight
into the orchard on a star-dark evening)

which will stick like stones to the earth's
skirt and whirl with her in dumb glory
until the seed warms and suddenly,
some hot other summer, using the scythe
to scatter and lay the loud weeds

to sour death beneath a yellowing sun . . .
I will lift my head and marvelously see
this soft young sapling, standing straight
as a young girl, there in the naughty boy briers,
full of her tender mother's fruity hope.

## Now on These Monuments Falls the Rain

Now on these monuments falls the rain,
careless oars plashing over words
which seem to hold their memories in pain,
but grip only ignorance of the name.

The rain rows in marches on the grass
and stones alike, beating like a pulse
upon the flowers, forgotten in some past
to celebrate the weather's brutal mass.

May the Lord, whose presence here is known
in anonymity of grass and stone
but does not shield our symbol from the ice
that glazes words, and may our Christ
whose shadow is not seen upon this mound
nor shielding of the rain's cold falling down . . .
may He from ice and frigid rain devise
comfort for the heart, where all death lies.

## Gravity's the Villain in This Piece

Gravity's the villain in this piece—
the laxness in the rose to slow decrease,
the tired instinct found within a man
for slumber at the noon . . . the dim plan
within the dog to lift his leg no more
and curl his brain around into his spoor.

Old men are apt to dream of being trees
and sprouting leaves from ears, and these
same leaves, no doubt, desire descent
into hard rock, and stones seek banishment
to air. All earthly things that yearn
to rise, tend sternly downward, turn
upon themselves and bite their minds
like mad dogs reeling. Upright signs
of growth are ever full of doubt,
and even children fill with dreams of not.

# The Mill

It stands dark and isolated in a kind of dream,
unreal; the water falls like maidenhair,
and the miller's flesh has soured like cream
to sounds of thunder, and turned to air.

The rock abutment is worn like an old tooth
to a wet, darker color; some beams lie washing,
thick with fronds of grass. Submerged in truth,
they blink behind a rain of minnows flashing.

The solid floor where the miller walked
and felt his body jar, hard weight against another,
has turned to jelly in the shallows, pocked
by grasses greener than the wood, and tougher.

Most of all I know is like this: gone or old.
The splinter in the flesh can melt like snow
before the heat inside the finger can turn cold.
All hard things strain to be the first to go.

The dream lasts; I've dreamed it over and over:
a picture polished dark as glass in stone.
Sometimes at night I hear the water roar,
or hear the miller pacing on the boards, alone.

## The People in These Houses

I'm not depressed, as I walk along this street,
by the age of these old houses; it's not their weight
of years that bothers me. The only vestiges
within their walls are of a material state:
wicker chairs, arthritic from thirty winters,
a sofa mildewed by the basement's weather,
and boxes filled with letters not worth saving.
I don't believe that here, in this stale climate,
ghosts live on to curse the merely living.
I fear another kind of curse that works inside,
worse than sin behind closed shutters,
that the people here are still more deeply haunted
by nothing, nothing in their hearts to hide.

## The Vulture

In the study of vultures, I
have been casual. Nevertheless,
I've watched them circling in the sky
an eighth of a mile up, more or less.

Too far away, they lose identity,
become no different from any other bird,
no likelier to stop your eye
than a raindrop or an idle word.

And too near . . . only this morning
I saw a vulture on a fence post.
He remained inert, as if my coming
were but the coming of another ghost.

Then he stirred, and I saw him drop
toward the ground and heard his pinions
clap as they caught the air; then up
he began to row to his old dominion.

For nobility, I had been too near.
That head was like an amputation wound,
and the expression in the eye was blear
as rotten ice blinded by the moon.

I've seen the black one far enough away
that there's nobility in his glide.
Up close, he crawls with lice, turns gray . . .
while vision feasts upon his carrion pride.

## After the Old Gods

In the dark inconsequence of night
a creature sometimes thrusts its snout
into a dream, as if to shove your knowledge out;
and sometimes ghosts of rats emerge to bite.

Not many of the pantheon you know from books
immerse themselves in that deep water
you swim through, numb in mind. Farther
than the Lethe of your sleep, they took

their shape from the unveined masses there
where you are darkest and most ignorant.
Their avatars are many: surly, bent
as rusted nails from rotted boards, they glare

like solder flaming in a crack of tin,
and then go out to harden cold as stone;
and yet the stuff they turn to looks like bone . . .
all substances are metaphors of skin.

## The Thaw

Icicles, which grow silently in the night,
crash glassily in the afternoon. I hear
them melting; hear the cracking
as they unfinger the eaves and, heavy as jugs,
plummet to the shining walks.
Sunlight is hot as summertime; it pries
the night-grip loose. Icy water
flashes beneath the hollow filigrees
of crusted snow, all canopied
on blades of grass. Through the footsteps
of swiftly stepping girls,
I see it trickling.

# The Old Man Next Door

Older, he grows more to hobbling
around the yard, while thoughts of business
shutter on and off more slowly in his mind,
like the details of an unclear dream.
It is the flowers that interest him now,
and the characteristics of grass.
They were all like children shouting
and playing about his feet for years;
but—preoccupied—he hadn't heard.

Until now. They had pushed their way
into light from all those stone-dead seeds,
silent as morning, underneath the soil
his feet press. I've seen him look
the other way, too—twenty minutes,
awed and unmoving, chin stretched up
as he squinted at the lineaments of sky
and wondered what had lured the flowers
and grass into these avenues of light.

## The Follower

I once plowed the leather turf of winter—
marched manly behind a horse bigger
than my father's shadow, stumbled
in the half-moon ditches of his hooves
and gazed in wonder at the swath
his might carved in an iron sod.

This great plangency of beast
has warped my world beyond adjustment.
Ever since, I've followed something
vast as weather, deep as birds,
which plods a way for me in time.

Sometimes I hear his presence loom in sleep,
and I stumble to my hands and knees;
I grope again in an ancient boyhood fear,
and feel in the clay those hooved craters,
the size of moonshards, where he's gone before.

## The Migrations

Signs there are of the old habitual change.
Standing in a field this evening, I looked up,
startled by silence; and there I saw
a thousand birds quieter than rain, flying.

Once as a child, I asked my father this:
"How can birds hear the cold nights coming?"
Now, thirty migrations later, I lament
the answer that he gave, for I've forgotten.

A simple thing like this, one asked at seven,
answered by my father then and there . . .
still, still the ghostly birds are flying
beyond my sight, beyond that child's consent.

## Toward a Greater Visibility

Pressed dumb in that dark and silent force
of ignorance, the seed still yearns toward air,
and reaches green into the slightest breach
of clay, as if it knew from memory of grain
what it's like to stand and lean away
from the warm, rain-heavy winds,
and feel the cool nights, drizzling stars,
drip like the silent side of light
upon the dark tassels and the leaves . . .
as if, pounded like a senseless nail into
the darkness of the clay, this uncouth seed
is pulled upward toward the sight of day,
as thoughts of Heaven, so the old ones say,
once lured ignorant men to foolish deeds.

# The Cheerleaders

Six girls in red skirts and red sweaters,
screaming by the field's pool table green
for the ghostly crowds on the grandstand hill
to print on silence their tumultuous will.

Six girls in short skirts and thick sweaters . . .
they are enthusiasms where thrilling dwells;
and in this dwelling, thrills almost love these
bright and sunny storms with hard and shiny knees.

What subsequence could justify such passion?
What happiness remains when the right team wins,
and the locker doors are closed, the boys sleeping,
and six silences lie in the midnight's keeping?

# The Ripeness of Winter

There comes a day when the snowbanks
go gray and soft, and the sun
is warm like the earliest light
in an April dawn. The drift shadows
turn dim from the glacial blue
of winter mornings,
and the whiteness of the fields
fades beneath the shadows
of a ragged cloud of birds.

Now the windows of the house
are raised grating against their frames
to let the sweet wind stir in the curtains.
Let us admit: the cold is such
that in November we would be surprised
at open windows—would close the house
and turn inward toward an open fire,
thumbing old books and blessing
all the sealed corners which nail in
warmth and the very breath we breathe.

But there is an over-ripeness here,
of winter and our mood. This house
has been itself too long; today
our hearts awake like cold flowers
that turn in silence toward the sun.

Open the windows, let the air wash
oldness from these rooms and halls.
The light now blows like robins on the snow;
the clouds of morning build a range of hills
with the shadows of rain; the breeze
is numb with warmth and smells of sun.

## Eros Oikoumenikos

No drunkenness like the drunkenness
of this. At the age of twenty, I
was versed in old theologies and sin.
Opposite, in ignorance, a girl's breast,
the secret warmth in a woman's thigh.

Phrases turned to eyes, hot flowers
to my hiving lust. For this fever,
I'd prescribed bleeding into the centuries
of men long turned to words; or even
an actual liquor to bring sobriety,
compared with this. There was no cure;
all things turned to metaphors of girls.

And I read this legend once: old Noah
survived the flood, the curse of drink,
and many a fearful, unnamed demon,
but when he drowned in his nine hundred
and fiftieth year, he drowned in woman.

## A Mother

It isn't until this restful evening
following her youngest son's marriage
that she begins to comb small spiders
out of her hair. The sun disintegrates
into a steaming rain . . . she gazes upon
a massive world without finch or robin
to spy tiny spiders. What gravity
can pull so heavily? A shard of moon
spins about her head . . . she sees stars
sticking to her fingers, the wind blackens,
and still the numberless, innocent spiders
tumble numbly over her pale and naked arms
as she combs, with her eyes tightly closed.

# Old Resort

The children hated everything about it.
The lake itself was full of furry logs
floating like dead bears beneath the surface.
The cabins along the shore were gray,
sweetly sickened by repose and silence.
The children felt a kind of fear
nudge at their knees when watchfully
they waded in the mossy shallows.

Great Aunt Maudie wets her hankie at the pump
and pastes it upon her eyes. Blindly smiling,
she eases the pressure of her heavy legs,
and lies supinely in her canvas chair.
She remembers the season fifty years before
and sighs: "How peaceful silence is!"

The children gaze out on the livid water,
and watch the sky grow stars within an hour.
Aunt Maudie snores; somewhere an oarlock
scratches, fumbles at an unmatched oar.
A baby cries and whimpers in the darkness,
at another cabin, on another shore.

# Montana Night at Twenty Below

The train stood whirring in the shuck of the mountain,
so massed above I could hear its hard walls,
abyssed with cold. The cheerful conductor,
old and ugly, hacked aboard
and told me that it was twenty below, that snow
was falling from the sky. I had just washed
and I was still stripped to the waist.
Ringing my head in cold water, I went outside,
half naked . . . twenty years old, at twenty below.
The snow reached over the track bed in the dark
to the weak, yellow lights of buildings, there
like stilled sparks in the blackened chimney of night,
caught up in the mountainous draft.
In all this, I was the bed that burned.
I was a furnace and I roared with fire inside.
My loneliness was fury, and my fury was hope.
Something did not like my sounds, it pressed
me away into minutes and hours . . . humbled me to time,
as if I had not been a god at all . . . as if
it had not seen the yet undoomed truth of my being
what I was in this unlikely shaft of stone and ice.
But I can remember what I was then, and how. . . .
I was a furnace and I roared with fire inside.

## A Preference in Women

Give me, for instance, a woman with shyness
and pain wrinkles webbed about her eyes;
the problem of weight, a certain
futility of age invested in her spine,
twisted stockings and the awkward
look of love surprised on her face
late in a sleepy evening.

## Old Canal Boat

Once it was towed like something half reluctant,
or gravid, gliding to this muddy mooring.
The stagnant water that sustained it once
has turned to sky. Now this rickety lair
stands hollowed of all sound.

The channel still remains—a gulley clotted
with ironweed and thistle dry as pollen.
The blackbirds flutter in the stems and dart
along old fish trails up the grassy ditch.

The lightness of the sun, soft drifting snow,
and rain as shy as breezes—these, the touch
of seasons, have corrupted this crude boat,
and now it lies unballasted of noise—
its squeaking progress up a hill of water,
towed by mules, whose neuter bones long since
have been the bread of gulley weed and clay.

# Two Gardens

There are two gardens;
one seen and one spoken,
one breathed and one heard.
In the two gardens are two meadowlarks;
one discovered, one figmented . . .
and each is each.

Swiftly, one garden is gone,
carrying its black-bibbed lark,
both of it, in a kind of breeze which blows
upon the memory, bringing odors
of one garden, one garden, one garden,
softly becoming one.

Where is the real garden we long for?
It flutters before us like a swift wing . . .
we see it only at the edges of its arc.

Such suddenness in the interchange of gardens—
such beauty in the word, the sound
of meadowlark upon a twig slender
as midnight, quivering the damp green leaves.

## Lecture for Last Meeting With Freshmen

Now, in this ceremonial
I face each year, and you
meet for the first and only time,
I am the one who is awed.

Would you believe me if I said
I've heard footsteps in the nights
snapping twigs as loud as chicken bones,
more mortal than my wrists and hair?

No, such a metaphor will not suffice,
for you are vacationing
in the most fictitious time of all
when everything is simply
what it seems to be.
But I can remember too many rooms
drowned like sunken ships
in the silent wash of years.

Or perhaps it is this way:
after many seasons, the voices
of coeds chatter like the rain,
anonymous as a crew of drunken birds
on a sweet spring night,
and the sound of a football
punted high into the hickory limbs
scatters no more leaves into air . . .
is heard now only as a heartbeat,
remembered, solitary, lost.

What do you remember of these things?
Do you think this poem through
and understand the pain of art?
Have you learned that metaphors
can turn to rock and sand,
and even to ancient buildings
if they have a mind?
Or that all things founder sadly,
even in their excellence?

As even now: the room yaws, flooded
by an old unballasting of days,
while one girl files her nails,
and stares out at the campus lawn,
anticipating summer joys;
and I stand here alone
at the turning hinge of one more year,
already remembering
this time,
and the similar faces that you wore.

# Remembered

We walked through puddles of black water,
still as cold coffee . . . felt the thread-thin rain
blister on our faces and in our hair . . .
walked the midnight to still sleep and talked
of God and chance and future . . . those days
of undergraduate concern, my sweet, have riddled
deep into my drowsing will, have become
the me I talk about when I am all alone.
Listen. I hear nightrain shake its air
and old November is cranking up to start.
This is our time. Remember? Always,
an earnest girl in a belted raincoat
is walking slowly toward me . . . her breath
is visible in the night, her loving palpable.
The lovely girl with tin drops of moisture
on her hairtips, and eyes that sound happy
in the drizzle, brings back thoughts of God
and chance and time's cold cheating,
and I hear you always speaking my single name
beneath the squeak of the rain's small wheels.

# Winter: Iron Tools in a Shed

It was born corrupted, hard
and dumb, pried into the light,
smelted by the fires
it hates, and poured
into the crooked molds of man;
stamped and pounded to the needs
of fools, it leans earthwards
in the cadence of a star-glint shed,
throughout the long disuse of winter,
homeward to that ancientness of rock.
Magnetized by darkness, it draws cold rime
and wears it like the furs of brutal kings,
when the workmen are least aware,
and slowly grows to rust.

# As From the Distance

There at the edge of distance, the river;
veined into by plural tributaries,
and sunken, heavy, into the soft earth
whose flatlands grow soft lakes of lilies.

Intense as if a dream this haunted scene.
I stood a child upon these shores and saw
it all as from the sky and heard the waves
lap like turning pages . . . felt the yaw

of heart blown wild into the river,
felt the ground pulse underneath my arm,
the mother wind blow lagging strings of rain
into my hair . . . remembered how a storm

gathered like a night beyond the shore,
and the blind lilies slanted from the wind
while the river spray arose like clouds
and wild as horses rode across the land.

Elemental as the day and night this scene.
I've blown like a torn shower through weed
and misted over miles of lily lakes,
where at dusk the shadowed heron feed.

And will blow to the rushing screeds of wind
like spray and stars all swirled together;
remember every element from dreams and know
all habitats are mine; there is no other.

# Backsight

Once glimpsing those quivering wires
which support the narrow fronts
of all stores—all commerce in this fast
and worried city—one can see
that what it's all about is not half worth
belief. The charade of edifices leaning
into our attention does not beguile
as once it did. All the ways of man
might clamor for our concern
and yet one cannot forget all
that trembling maze of guys, of props
behind buildings which flash
in the artificial light. See the windows—
scattered pools of rain in a vacant field.

# Anatomy Lesson

Men are made of mostly space
and lean on air as on a crutch;
I've examined the densest place—
of hate, perhaps, or love—and there
the fact eludes the mind's clutch,
for inside every heart is air.

I know that nothing like a book.
It's what we crave; I knew a fool
who concentrated on the Truth
until his falsehood sifted out
and left him there an empty tool.
The Truth was interstellar space,
snug as a cavity in his tooth.
They took a picture of it then—
a time exposure made at dawn;
they came at night and made the print,
which was pure light; the man was gone.

# The Awake

It is now, in the dark heaviness of the spruce swamp,
barred like a brassy cage, silent as water, that the bear
licks at his heart beat, the old buck lies panting
to lose a hard day's growth of antler in his brain.

It is now that mice leisurely restore themselves
under rotten stumps, that elm trees drink black space,
and wheat flattens like wind on the darkened earth.
Men sigh and mumble in their covers; women knit at dreams.

Let us pity those who are left to listen to that old noise
of the moon as it's cranked high into the hollow sky.

## The Second Growth

Old Silas Smith, you settled on this land
after riding your horse through forests
as dark and damp as lake bottoms,
and carving from its heart fields
with your own hard hands.

Like God, you cleared the chaos, making light
for the growth of crops and sons.
Now we are settlers of a different night;
that wilderness you conquered grows
more dark and tangled here inside our hearts,
a hostile land where we ax row on row
of trees to clear a place for a human site.

# The Awful One

"He is the old man who loses his temper!"
the children cry. All-frowning,
he swaddles them in Jovian thunder
and with his jaw chops words
to fall among them like tall pines
axed in a dim, amber twilight.

The children explode before him like sparrows
unflocked by a wild stone thrown,
but always they return to his thorny edge of rage
to watch him with jewels in their eyes.

For there is no one on the whole block
whom they prize more; these dirty, tender children.

# Afterthought at Evening

Now, even tag changes;
and touched by stranger hands,
the children shout and laugh,

and fireflies pulse uneven in the dark
like cigarettes in the breezy mouths
of unseen watchers on the lawn.

And all this time, the children know
the windows are filled with light,
showing where parents sit and talk.

What if in the midst of play,
the parents should depart
silently, and the house go dark?

# Alum Creek

Not only the wading in the dark shallows,
walking the heron's quiet floor to emerge
in the wide placidness and splash heavily
through the water, to the sycamore roots,
and back into the sun-bronzed deeps. . . .
not only this, was our joy in Alum's waters,
but the standing naked on the hot shale, shaded
by a humming web of limbs and leaves.
There, scrubbed and lengthened by an hour,
we lighted cigarettes and leisurely burned
leeches from our toes in pensive absolution.
Then, we pulled socks on our shale-dusted feet
and inhaled summer into our memories.

## Herd of Bison

And still appear to move, wandering in a stream—
ungainly, shaggy, proud. The king bulls raise
their heads, each head a bush of thorns. The strays
circle the herd, moving slowly through a dream.
The bison settle down like silence, and a star
is mirrored, one for one, in each dumb eye.
Here and there in the darkness, a calf will cry,
struck by a dim odor of space and where they are . . .
ignorant child, confounded by a language, crossed
by a wind that tells his heart that he is lost—
and all the herd as well. This alone, their hour
of meaning: glories of the knee-deep grasses,
flowers and wind—all that is loved passes.

## The Peace the Mind Turns To

Beneath devising, the mind pivots
upon silence, yearns toward the pivot,
not oblivion, which is the shadow
of silence, but that quiet point
whereon we turn, move and stay . . .
calm as a glass sea at evening,
alive as the robin's eye.